MW01490945

GENEVA TRAVEL GUIDE

2023 - 2024

The Your Ideal Vacation Guide To Geneva: An Informative Guide For Any One Planning a Trip to Geneva With Complete Essential Tips & 7 Days Expert Itinerary

BY

William Jose

GENEVA

TRAVEL GUIDE

2023 - 2024

WILLIAM JOSE

TABLE OF CONTENTS

INTRODUCTION

Geneva, sometimes known as the "Capital of Peace," is a gorgeous city in the center of Switzerland. Geneva is a genuinely amazing place that encapsulates the spirit of Swiss refinement and global diplomacy, with a rich history, spectacular natural beauty, and a worldwide reputation.

The city is located at the southern extremity of Lake Geneva, surrounded by snow-capped mountains and picturesque scenery. Because of its scenic surroundings, Geneva is a fantastic destination for outdoor enthusiasts and nature lovers. The famed Jet d'Eau, a majestic water fountain that sprays water 140 meters into the air, is a must-see sight and an iconic emblem of the city.

Geneva is widely regarded as a diplomatic and peacekeeping hotspot. Numerous international organizations call it home, including the European headquarters of the United Nations and the Red Cross. The city's dedication to diplomatic and humanitarian activities is reflected in its many museums, including as the International Red Cross and Red Crescent Museum, which give insight into the world's current concerns and attempts to solve them.

Vieille Ville, or Old Town, is a lovely region with small cobblestone alleys, old buildings, and a lively ambiance. St. Peter's Cathedral, a magnificent gothic-style monument dating back to the 12th century, may be explored here. The Old Town also has charming cafés, boutique stores, and art galleries, making it ideal for a leisurely walk and a taste of Swiss culture.

Geneva has a fantastic collection of museums and galleries for anyone interested in art and culture. The Musée d'Art et d'Histoire holds a large collection of art, archaeology, and applied arts, whilst the Patek Philippe Museum exhibits the history of horology and fine watches. The Grand Théâtre de Genève is well-known for its world-class opera and ballet performances, which draw art lovers from all over the world.

Geneva is also a gastronomic destination, with a wide variety of restaurants serving both traditional Swiss cuisine and cosmopolitan influences. The city's closeness to France has had an impact on its cuisine, resulting in a delectable blend of French and Swiss culinary traditions. Visitors may savor Swiss cheese fondue, decadent chocolate, and fine wines while taking in stunning views of the lake and the Alps.

Finally, Geneva is a mesmerizing city that blends natural beauty, cultural legacy, and worldwide relevance in a seamless manner. Whether you're attracted to Geneva by its gorgeous landscapes, its position in international diplomacy, or its bustling cultural and culinary scene, every visitor will have a one-of-a-kind and memorable experience.

Brief History of Geneva

Geneva, Switzerland, has a rich and intriguing history dating back thousands of years. Its strategic position at the convergence of the Rhône River and Lake Geneva has shaped its future significantly. The region surrounding Geneva has been populated from ancient times, including traces of Neolithic towns. It was a bustling commercial hub known as "Geneva" in Roman times and subsequently became a significant center of Christianity throughout the early medieval era.

Geneva became a free city and experienced a period of relative freedom throughout the Middle Ages. However, under the leadership of John Calvin, the city became a major center of the Protestant Reformation in the 16th century. Calvin's influence converted Geneva into a Protestant think center and a destination for religious refugees from all across Europe.

In the centuries since, Geneva has played an important role in European diplomacy and international affairs. It grew into a commerce and financial center, drawing merchants and bankers from all across the continent. The city has developed a reputation as a center for intellectual and scientific investigation, with noteworthy residents like Jean-Jacques Rousseau and Voltaire.

The nineteenth century saw substantial political developments in Geneva. In 1815, it joined the Swiss Confederation and underwent significant industrialisation. The International Committee of the Red Cross, based in Geneva, established the city's image as a hub of humanitarianism and peace in 1863. Geneva continued to play an important role in international politics throughout the twentieth century. In 1946, it became the United Nations' European headquarters, housing various international organizations and holding crucial diplomatic talks. The city has seen historic events such as the signing of the Geneva Conventions and the staging of different peace negotiations.

Geneva has become a worldwide financial, diplomatic, and scientific hub. It is well-known for its high standard of living, cultural variety, and dedication to human rights. The attractive location of the city, with the breathtaking background of the Alps and Lake Geneva, draws travelers from all over the globe.

Geneva's history is a patchwork of religious, political, and intellectual influences that have molded the city's distinct personality. Geneva, from its modest beginnings as a Roman trade station to its current position as a cosmopolitan city, has thrived as a beacon of international collaboration and innovation.

Population And People of Geneva

Geneva, Switzerland's second most populous city, with a population of around 203,000 people. Geneva draws a varied population and adds to its cosmopolitan environment due to its international diplomacy and hosting of many organizations such as the United Nations and the Red Cross.

The city's population is a cultural melting pot, with people of all origins and ethnicities coexisting together. The city's appeal is enhanced by its variety, as inhabitants and tourists alike are exposed to a wide range of languages, cultures, and opinions. Genevans appreciate this global tapestry, creating an inclusive society in which everyone feels cherished and respected.

Geneva's pleasant and helpful citizens reflect the city's warm welcome. Locals are well-known for their courtesy, openness, and readiness to help others. Whether you're a tourist looking for instructions or a newbie looking for support, the people of Geneva are always ready to provide a kind smile and a helpful hand.

In conclusion, Geneva's population reflects the city's inclusive ethos, and the city's warm welcome makes it a very welcoming destination.

Geneva's Religious Practice

Geneva, Switzerland, is recognized for its diversified religious landscape and rich religious heritage. The city has served as a focal point for many religious groups and is home to a number of religious communities. Here are some of Geneva's prominent religious practices:

Christianity is the prevalent religion in Geneva, with both Protestantism and Catholicism having a large influence.

Protestantism: Geneva was a key player in the Protestant Reformation, and it is sometimes referred to as "Protestant Rome." The city is intimately identified with John Calvin, a pivotal figure in the Protestant Reformation whose views had a significant effect on the development of Reformed Christianity. This historical event is commemorated by the Reformation Wall, which is situated in Parc des Bastions. Throughout the city, there are several Protestant churches, notably St. Pierre Cathedral, which is intimately associated with Calvin's legacy.

Catholicism: While the bulk of Geneva's population is Protestant, the city also has a Catholic component. The Catholic Church is present in Geneva via different parishes and churches, and the Basilica of Notre-Dame is a significant Catholic monument.

Judaism: Geneva has a long history of Jewish community, and Jewish religious activity may be found across the city.

Synagogues: The Jewish community in Geneva is served by many synagogues, including Synagogue Beth Yaacov and Synagogue Beth Israel. Regular worship services, religious study, and cultural activities are held in these synagogues.

Islam: Geneva has a sizable Muslim community, and Islam is one of the city's major faiths.

Mosques: The Muslim community in Geneva is served by many mosques. The Grand Mosque of Geneva is one of the city's biggest and most visible mosques. It hosts Friday prayers, Islamic education, and a variety of community events.

Other faiths: In addition to the main faiths described above, Geneva has a number of other religious groups and customs.

Buddhism: Buddhist temples and organizations in Geneva provide meditation sessions, lectures, and cultural activities.

Hinduism: There are Hindu temples and organizations in Geneva that cater to the religious and cultural requirements of the Hindu population.

different religions: Because Geneva is an international city, you may discover devotees of a variety of different religions and religious practices, such as Sikhism, the Bahá' Faith, and others.

It is crucial to note that religious practices differ amongst people and communities within Geneva, and this overview gives a basic idea of the city's main religious organizations and their existence.

Chapter One

Transit Options And The Cost of Getting To Geneva, The Tourist Center Of Peace

Traveling to Geneva is an amazing experience that wakes the senses and inspires an adventurous attitude. This cosmopolitan city, nestled in the majestic Swiss Alps, offers a wonderful mix of natural beauty, rich history, and dynamic culture. The mere prospect of wandering along Lake Geneva's immaculate shoreline, staring at the spectacular Jet d'Eau, and discovering the picturesque Old Town excites one's heart. Geneva is a sensory joy at every turn, from strolling through the scenic streets lined with fine stores to indulging in scrumptious Swiss chocolate. The international ambience of the city, with its various organizations and diplomatic institutions, provides a sophisticated aura. Geneva encourages guests to embark on a trip that offers exceptional moments and a thrilling escape from the mundane, with its breathtaking landscapes, cultural riches, and tangible aura of tranquility.

Air Travel To Geneva

The cost of air travel may vary based on a number of variables, including the departure location, airline, time of booking, and travel dates. The table below shows some samples of air travel expenses from several cities to Geneva, Switzerland. Please keep in mind that all costs are estimates and subject to change.

From London, England to Geneva, Switzerland:

Low-cost carriers such as easyJet and Ryanair: one-way tickets start at $50-100 USD.
Full-service carriers such as British Airways and Swiss International Air Lines: $150-300 USD (one-way).

From Paris to Geneva, Switzerland:
Low-cost carriers such as easyJet and Transavia: one-way tickets start at $50-100 USD.
Full-service carriers such as Air France and Swiss International Air Lines: $150-300 USD (one-way).

From Frankfurt in Germany to Geneva in Switzerland:

Low-cost carriers such as Ryanair and Eurowings: one-way tickets start at $50-100 USD.

Full-service carriers such as Lufthansa and Swiss International Air Lines: $150-300 USD (one-way)

From New York City to Geneva, Switzerland: Full-service carriers such as Delta Air Lines, United carriers, and Swiss International Air Lines: round-trip tickets start at $500-800 USD.

Prices might vary greatly depending on the time of year, with peak travel seasons being typically more costly.

From Dubai in the United Arab Emirates to Geneva in Switzerland: Full-service carriers such as Emirates and Swiss International Air Lines: round-trip tickets start at $600-900 USD.

Prices fluctuate according to season and demand.

Land Travel to Geneva

Land travel alternatives and expenses to Geneva from various areas might vary based on distance, method of conveyance, and availability. Here are some frequent starting places for land travel to Geneva, as well as estimated costs:

Traveling by land from Zurich, Switzerland: Rail: A direct rail ride from Zurich to Geneva takes roughly 2.5

hours and costs between 50 and 100 CHF (Swiss Francs) for a one-way ticket, depending on the type of train and ticket class.

Driving from Zurich to Geneva takes around 280 kilometers (175 miles) and takes 3-4 hours, depending on traffic. Fuel and tolls may be charged.

Traveling by land from Paris, France: Train: High-speed trains (TGV) run between Paris and Geneva, taking around 3-4 hours. A one-way ticket costs between 50 and 150 EUR (Euros), depending on the train and class.

Bus: Several bus companies provide service between Paris and Geneva. Travel duration may range from 6 to 8 hours, and ticket costs range from 20 to 50 EUR, depending on the operator and time of purchase.

Traveling by land from Milan, Italy: Train: Direct trains link Milan and Geneva and take around 3-4 hours. One-way train tickets normally cost between 20 and 60 EUR, depending on the train and class.

Car: The drive from Milan to Geneva is about 315 kilometers (195 miles) and takes around 3.5-4.5 hours, depending on traffic conditions and route. Fuel and tolls may be charged.

Traveling by land from Munich, Germany: Traveling by rail from Munich to Geneva normally necessitates a transfer, and the overall travel duration might range between 6 and 8 hours. Depending on the train and class, one-way tickets run from 50 to 100 EUR.

Car: The distance between Munich and Geneva is around 550 kilometers (340 miles), and the drive takes approximately 5-7 hours, depending on traffic and route. Fuel and tolls may be charged.

It's crucial to remember that these rates are estimates and may change depending on variables including trip dates, booking times, and discounts.

Sea Travel To Geneva

Because Geneva is a landlocked city in Switzerland, traveling by water is not an option. Although the city is located on the shores of Lake Geneva, it does not have direct access to the sea. As a result, no one can go by water to Geneva from anywhere.

However, if you are seeking alternate means to go to Geneva, you might try using the air or road, as previously discussed.

Month by Month Weather in Geneva

January - February

Geneva receives chilly and icy weather in January and February. During these months, the average temperature fluctuates between -2°C (28°F) and 5°C (41°F). Snowfall is frequent, particularly in the city's higher altitudes and hilly surroundings. The days are often short and have little sunshine, while the nights may be rather cold.

January is traditionally the coldest month, with temperatures falling below freezing. Snow blankets the ground, creating a beautiful winter scene. To keep comfortable outside, wear warm clothes with numerous layers, including caps, gloves, scarves, and thick jackets.

The weather gradually shifts towards spring in February. While temperatures remain low, warmer days with temperatures around 5°C (41°F) are possible. Snowfall is still possible, and tourists should be prepared for changing weather conditions.

Overall, January and February in Geneva provide a full winter experience, with snowy landscapes and a comfortable ambiance, making it a popular period for winter sports enthusiasts and those looking for a peaceful winter retreat.

March - April

Geneva transitions from winter to spring between March and April, with noteworthy shifts in weather patterns. With average temperatures ranging from 2°C (36°F) to 11°C (52°F), March maintains some winter qualities. Snowfall is possible, although it will become less common as the month develops. April brings warmer weather, with temperatures ranging from 5°C (41°F) to 15°C (59°F). As the days lengthen and spring blossoms appear, the atmosphere becomes more vivid. While rain is forecast during both months, April is often wetter. It's a period of seasonal transition and growing excitement for the warmer months ahead.

May - June

Geneva sees the shift from spring to early summer between May and June. May temperatures range from 12 to 21 degrees Celsius (54 to 70 degrees Fahrenheit) while June temperatures range from 15 to 24 degrees Celsius (59 to 75 degrees Fahrenheit). Rainfall is light, with a few showers and some sunny days. While visiting the city at this period, bring light clothing and a rain jacket. The lovely Lake Geneva provides a lovely background for outdoor activities.

July - August

The weather in Geneva, Switzerland, is typically pleasant and warm in July and August, with average high temperatures ranging from 24°C (75°F) to 28°C (82°F). July is the hottest month, with highs of 32°C (90°F) on rare occasions. Evenings are typically colder, with temperatures falling to roughly 15°C (59°F). Rainfall is moderate, with showers and thunderstorms on occasion. Temperatures drop somewhat in August, with highs averaging approximately 25°C (77°F). During these months, the city receives a considerable quantity of sunlight, offering abundant chances for outdoor activities and sightseeing. Pack lightweight, breathable clothes, as well as an umbrella or raincoat in case of unexpected rainfall.

September - October

Geneva transitions from summer to autumn between September and October. With typical daytime temperatures ranging from 15 to 20 degrees Celsius (59 to 68 degrees Fahrenheit), the weather progressively cools. It is normally moderate, with just sporadic rain. The days begin to shorten, and the foliage changes, producing a gorgeous fall ambiance. To adjust to changing weather conditions, it is best to carry a combination of light and warm clothes.

November - October

In November and December, the weather in Geneva is often chilly and snowy. Temperatures range between 3°C (37°F) and 9°C (48°F) during the day and drop to 0°C (32°F) or lower at night, marking the transition from autumn to winter. Throughout the month, the city receives a lot of rain, which is frequently accompanied by high gusts. Temperatures continue to fall as December approaches, with typical daytime highs of approximately 3°C (37°F) and overnight lows of -2°C (28°F). Snowfall becomes increasingly common, particularly in the second half of December, converting Geneva into a gorgeous winter wonderland. It is important to wrap up and wear properly at this time of year since the weather may be extremely frigid. Despite the cold, Geneva's attractiveness remains intact, and the city provides a variety of festive events and activities, making it an ideal holiday vacation.

Chapter Two

Geneva Travel Preparation

Preparation is essential before going to Geneva, or any other place, to guarantee a smooth and pleasurable journey.

Best Time To Visit Geneva

The finest seasons to visit Geneva are in the spring (April to June) and autumn (September to October). The weather is normally moderate during these times, with temperatures ranging from 10 to 20 degrees Celsius (50 to 68 degrees Fahrenheit). During the spring, the city is in full bloom, with magnificent flowers and budding trees adding to its allure.

Geneva has beautiful fall foliage throughout the autumn, creating a charming ambiance. These seasons also have fewer tourists than the peak summer months and winter ski season, enabling visitors to explore the city and its attractions with more ease.

Throughout the year, Geneva also organizes a number of recognized events and festivals. Popular events include the

Geneva International Motor Show in March and the Geneva Festival in July. With various museums, galleries, restaurants, and cafés to visit, the city's unique cultural and gastronomic scene may be enjoyed all year.

In conclusion, visiting Geneva in the spring or fall gives good weather, less people, and the chance to explore the city's dynamic culture and activities.

Geneva's Neighborhoods City Tour

Geneva is a lovely city with a variety of intriguing areas to discover. Here's a recommended city tour of some of Geneva's most noteworthy neighborhoods:

Old Town (Vieille Ville): Begin your visit at Geneva's Old Town. Explore its tiny, charming alleyways dotted with old structures, boutiques, and cafés. Climb the tower of St. Peter's Cathedral, a spectacular architectural icon, for panoramic views of the city and Lake Geneva.

Place du Bourg-de-Four: One of Geneva's oldest squares is Place du Bourg-de-Four. Cafes, restaurants, and retailers surround this busy plaza. Take time to unwind and enjoy the lively environment.

Carouge: A short tram trip will take you to Carouge, a beautiful district with an Italian flavor. Explore the lively alleys lined with artisan shops, art galleries, and cafés. Don't miss the Carouge Market, which sells fresh food, flowers, and regional specialities.

Eaux-Vives: To get to the Eaux-Vives area, walk along Lake Geneva's magnificent promenade. This neighborhood has a variety of green areas, fashionable pubs, and eateries. Take a walk around the lakeside and enjoy the Jet d'Eau, one of Geneva's most recognizable sights.

Paquis: Continue your journey to the Paquis area, which is recognized for its cosmopolitan atmosphere. Visit the lively Rue de Paquis, which is teeming with foreign restaurants, cafés, and stores. Enjoy the stunning views of the lake by walking along the Quai du Mont-Blanc.

Nations: Go to the Nations neighborhood to discover the United Nations Office and other international institutions. Visit Ariana Park and the Palais des Nations for a guided tour of the United Nations headquarters.

Plainpalais: The journey concludes in Plainpalais, a lively and stylish district. Visit the Plainpalais Flea Market, which is held every Wednesday and Saturday and sells vintage products, antiques, and local crafts. Discover the Reformation Wall and the famed enormous chessboard at the Parc des Bastions.

This city trip will introduce you to Geneva's numerous neighborhoods, each with their own distinct charm and attractions. Have fun exploring the city!

Transit Options Of Exploring Geneva Neighborhood

Typically, transit ways of touring a neighborhood relate to numerous forms of transportation that may be utilized to traverse and discover diverse regions.

Here are some popular modes of transportation and their associated costs:

Walking is a cheap and ecologically beneficial method to get about an area. It enables you to take your time exploring the surroundings. However, when compared to other modes of transportation, the range and pace of investigation are restricted.

Bicycles: When compared to walking, bicycles allow a speedier and more broad range of exploration. The fee varies depending on whether you own or rent a bicycle. If you currently own a bike, the costs are mostly upkeep and any required repairs. If you decide to hire a bicycle, the cost will vary based on the length of the rental and the location.

Public transit, such as buses, trams, or subways, is a popular and inexpensive method to explore an area. The rates vary depending on the city and the distance traveled. Some cities give single-ride tickets, day passes, or weekly/monthly passes at reduced prices for regular riders.

Ride-Sharing Services: Ride-sharing services such as Uber and Lyft are handy ways to explore a new area. They provide door-to-door service, with prices determined by criteria such as distance, time, and demand. Prices may vary during peak hours or in high-demand locations.

Car Rentals: Renting a car gives you greater freedom and independence while exploring a new area. Car rental prices vary based on the rental agency, kind of vehicle, rental term, and any extra services such as insurance. Fuel expenditures should be addressed as well.

Guided Tours: In famous tourist sites, guided tours are often provided and give a systematic approach to see a neighborhood. These excursions may be taken on foot, by bus, or on specialized vehicles such as Segways. The pricing will vary depending on the tour operator and the length of the excursion.

Geneva Entry Requirements

Switzerland, including Geneva, is a part of the Schengen Area, which enables people of numerous countries to travel visa-free for short-term vacation, business, or family trips. You do not need a visa to visit Switzerland if you are a citizen of one of the Schengen Area member nations.

A visa is necessary for nationals of countries outside the Schengen Area, including the United States, Canada, Australia, and many more. The kind of visa and application procedure are determined by your nationality, purpose of travel, and length of stay.

To find out whether you need a visa and the exact criteria, contact the Swiss embassy or consulate in your home country. They will provide you with the most up-to-date and correct information. Alternatively, you may go to the official website of Switzerland's State Secretariat for Migration (SEM).

Aside from visa restrictions, you may be subject to the following general regulations while entering Switzerland, including Geneva:

Passport: Make sure your passport is valid for at least three months beyond the date of your intended trip.

Evidence of lodging: It is recommended that you have documentation of your lodging arrangements, such as hotel bookings or an invitation letter from a host if you are staying with someone.

Sufficient funds: You may be asked to present evidence that you have enough money to support your stay in Switzerland. Bank statements, credit cards, and cash are all examples.

Return ticket: It is suggested that you have a return or onward ticket to demonstrate your intention to depart Switzerland within the time range specified.

Travel insurance: It is a good idea to get travel insurance that covers medical expenditures and repatriation.

Stay duration

It is advised that you spend at least 5 to 7 days in Geneva as a visitor to completely immerse yourself in its rich cultural and scenic offers. Begin with a visit to the famed Jet d'Eau and a walk around Lake Geneva's gorgeous shoreline. Explore the Old Town's ancient beauty by strolling around its small alleyways and visiting St. Pierre Cathedral. Visit world-class institutions such as the Red Cross Museum and the Museum of Art and History. Indulge in the gastronomic delicacies of the city, such as Swiss chocolates and cheese fondue. Don't miss the lively retail center, and for a day trip, take a boat to neighboring Montreux.

Geneva Travel Essentials

There are a few packing items you should consider taking with you while going to Geneva, Switzerland. Here's a list of products that can come in handy during your trip:

Clothing: Because Geneva enjoys a wide variety of temperatures throughout the year, bring clothing appropriate for the season of your stay. Layers are essential since the weather might change suddenly. Pack lightweight attire for the summer, such as t-shirts, shorts, and comfortable walking shoes. Bring warm sweaters, coats, caps, gloves, and a decent pair of boots in the winter.

Travel adaptor: Switzerland utilizes Type J electrical outlets, so pack a travel adaptor if you're coming from another country with a different plug type.

Passport, travel insurance papers, and any other relevant identity or travel documents should be carried. Having both physical and digital copies of these papers is a smart idea.

Money & Payment Methods: The Geneva currency is the Swiss Franc (CHF). Bring some cash for modest purchases, but a credit or debit card is highly recommended for bigger purchases. Inform your bank of your trip intentions in order to prevent problems with card use while overseas.

Comfortable Walking Shoes: Geneva is a walking city, so you'll probably spend most of your time exploring on foot. Pack comfortable walking shoes or sneakers to help you traverse the city's streets and attractions.

Rain Gear: Geneva sees rain all year, so bring a light umbrella or a waterproof jacket to remain dry during unexpected rains.

Medications and toiletries: If you need prescription drugs, make sure you pack enough for your vacation. It's also a good idea to bring along basic amenities like a toothbrush, toothpaste, and other personal care products you may require.

Bring a reusable water bottle to remain hydrated during the day, since Switzerland offers great tap water. This also aids in the reduction of plastic waste.

Evaluate any activities or events you want to attend and pack appropriately.

Chapter Three

Must See Top Geneva Attractions and Recreational Activities

Geneva, Switzerland has a wide range of outstanding attractions and leisure opportunities. Begin by seeing the stunning Jet d'Eau, a majestic water fountain on Lake Geneva. The renowned St. Pierre Cathedral is worth a visit for its spectacular architecture and panoramic views from the tower. Take a leisurely walk around Lake Geneva's lovely promenades or take a boat excursion to appreciate the surrounding beauty. Discover Old Town's beauty with its cobblestone streets, small shops, and historic sites. Enjoy world-class shopping on Rue du Rhône and delectable Swiss chocolate. Finally, relax in the quiet serenity of the Jardin Anglais or cool down in Bains des Pâquis.

Geneva Top Attractions You Must Not Miss

There are various major attractions in Geneva that you should not miss if you visit. Here are some of Geneva's must-see attractions:

The Jet d'Eau water fountain is one of Geneva's most recognizable monuments. It blasts water 140 meters into the air and serves as a municipal icon.

St. Pierre Cathedral: St. Pierre Cathedral, located in the Old Town, is an outstanding medieval cathedral with spectacular views from its towers. You may also investigate the cathedral's past by visiting the archaeological site underneath it.

Geneva's lovely Old Town, with its tiny, winding alleyways, gorgeous squares, and ancient buildings, is worth a walk. It's a fantastic area to explore and unearth hidden treasures.

Geneva is home to a number of international institutions, including the United Nations Office. A guided tour is available to learn about the work done there and to visit essential meeting areas.

Palace of Nations: The Palace of Nations is the European headquarters of the United Nations, and it is another prominent international institution in Geneva. Explore the majestic structure and its lovely surroundings on a guided tour.

Jardin Anglais: This lakefront park is popular with both residents and tourists. It has lovely flower beds, a renowned flower clock, and breathtaking views of Lake Geneva and the Jet d'Eau.

The Patek Philippe Museum should not be missed if you are interested in horology. It has an extraordinary collection of watches, timepieces, and automata from across history.

The Museum of Natural History, located in Parc de la Grange, provides intriguing displays on natural history, including animals, fossils, minerals, and more.

The International Red Cross and Red Crescent Museum teaches about the humanitarian efforts of the Red Cross and Red Crescent movements. It explores the history and values of these organizations via interactive exhibitions.

Carouge is recognized for its Italian-inspired architecture, colorful buildings, and lively environment. Explore the charming streets, shop at local shops, and dine at cafés and restaurants.

These are just a handful of Geneva's major attractions. The city has a rich cultural legacy, beautiful natural settings, and a number of museums and attractions to visit. Have a great time!

Who Should Visit Geneva

Geneva is a city with a diverse selection of sights and activities, making it appealing to a broad spectrum of tourists. Here are some groups of persons that could appreciate a trip to Geneva:

Enthusiasts of History and Culture: Geneva has a rich history and is renowned as the birthplace of the Red Cross as well as the hub of the Reformation. History aficionados may visit St. Pierre Cathedral, Maison Tavel (Geneva's oldest residence), and several museums that highlight the city's cultural legacy.

Diplomats and International Organizations: Geneva is a significant diplomatic center as well as the headquarters of several international organizations, including the United Nations, World Health Organization (WHO), International Red Cross, and World Trade Organization (WTO).

Diplomats, government officials, and international relations experts often visit Geneva for conferences, meetings, and diplomatic missions.

Nature Lovers: Geneva, located on the lovely beaches of Lake Geneva and bordered by the Alps, has breathtaking natural beauty. Visitors may take leisurely walks along the lake promenade, go on boat tours, or go hiking, skiing, and other outdoor sports in the adjacent countryside.

Food and Wine Lovers: Geneva is well-known for its gastronomic scene, which combines Swiss and foreign cuisines. Visitors may sample traditional Swiss cuisine, sample beautiful chocolates, and stroll through the city's colorful food markets. Geneva is also adjacent to the famed Swiss vineyards, giving it an ideal starting point for wine connoisseurs embarking on wine excursions.

Luxury Shoppers: Geneva is associated with luxury, and it is home to a plethora of high-end shops and jewelry stores. The city's Rue du Rhône is recognized for its upscale stores that sell famous Swiss watch brands, designer apparel, and fine jewelry.

Art and music lovers will enjoy Geneva's booming arts and music scene, which includes various galleries, museums, and theaters. The Grand Théâtre de Genève presents opera and ballet events, while the Museum of Art and History displays a wide variety of artworks.

Business Travelers: Geneva is a worldwide business and financial hub that attracts professionals from a wide range of sectors. The city hosts several conferences, trade fairs, and business events, making it an attractive location for business tourists.

Of course, they are not comprehensive, and Geneva can accommodate practically every sort of guest. Geneva's unique combination of history, nature, international relevance, and cultural attractions make it an enticing destination for a broad spectrum of people, whether for business, pleasure, or adventure.

Fun Adventure Activities For Tourists

Tourists may enjoy a variety of interesting adventure activities in Geneva, Switzerland. Here are some of the finest experiences you may have in Geneva:

Paragliding allows you to soar through the skies and enjoy spectacular views of Lake Geneva and the neighboring Alps. Tandem paragliding flights are available from many providers, enabling you to enjoy this exhilarating sport even if you have no previous expertise.

Jet Boating: Take a high-speed trip on Lake Geneva in a jet boat. Hold on tight as the boat zooms over the lake, spinning, turning, and completing exhilarating maneuvers. This heart-racing exercise is guaranteed to get your blood pounding.

Canyoning: Take a canyoning trip in the local mountains. Rappel down waterfalls, slide down natural rock slides, and splash into crystal-clear pools. Canyoning is an exciting and one-of-a-kind way to appreciate the natural splendor of the Swiss Alps.

Way Ferrata: A way ferrata is a mix of trekking and climbing. You'll use metal rungs, ladders, and cables to follow a secure path up a cliff face while wearing a harness and safety equipment. As you ascend the mountain, you will be rewarded with breathtaking vistas and a feeling of achievement.

Stand-Up Paddleboarding (SUP): Try stand-up paddleboarding for a peaceful trip on Lake Geneva. Rent a paddleboard and take your time exploring the quiet seas. It's a terrific way to unwind, take in the landscape, and get in some low-impact exercise.

Mountain Biking: Geneva is surrounded by wonderful mountain paths, making it a mountain biker's heaven. Rent a mountain bike and tackle the slopes to discover the breathtaking scenery and difficult terrain. There are alternatives for cyclists of all ability levels, from novice to expert.

Visit a tree-top adventure park, such as the Adventure Park Geneva, where you may maneuver through numerous obstacles, zip lines, and rope courses hung high in the trees. It's a fun and demanding exercise that's appropriate for both children and adults.

Hiking: Geneva has a variety of hiking paths for people of all fitness levels. Hike through the Jura Mountains or enjoy the lovely pathways surrounding Lake Geneva. You'll be rewarded with spectacular vistas, fresh air, and the chance to reconnect with nature.

45

Remember to confirm availability and safety measures with local tour operators and suppliers. Have a great time in Geneva!

Festivals and events that should not be missed

Geneva, Switzerland has a thriving cultural scene and holds a number of festivals and events throughout the year. Here are some must-see Geneva festivals and events:

1: The Geneva foreign Film Festival (November) features a broad range of foreign films, including documentaries, shorts, and feature films. It draws filmmakers, industry experts, and moviegoers from all around the globe.

2: The Geneva Music Festival (June to August) presents a variety of classical music events with notable performers and ensembles. The event is held in a variety of locations across the city, including music halls, churches, and outdoor places.

3: Montreux Jazz Festival (July): While not located in Geneva, the Montreux Jazz Festival is a world-renowned event hosted at a short distance away. It includes performances by both renowned and developing musicians in jazz, blues, rock, and pop music. The event, which takes place on the beaches of Lake Geneva, draws music fans from all over the world.

4: Geneva Festival (August): This colorful festival, which lasts a week, is one of the most important events in Geneva. Live music concerts, street performances, fireworks displays, food booths, and a big parade are among the many events available. The event is held along the beaches of Lake Geneva as well as at other sites across the city.

5: Fête de l'Escalade (December): This historic celebration recalls the Duke of Savoy's unsuccessful attempt to attack Geneva in 1602. The celebration includes reenactments, parades, costumed characters, traditional music, and delectable chocolate cauldrons known as "marmite," which are shattered and divided among attendees.

6: Geneva Marathon for Unicef (May): The Geneva Marathon provides a wonderful chance for sports enthusiasts to participate in a spectacular run around Lake Geneva. The race durations range from a full marathon to shorter fun runs, drawing both amateur and professional runners.

7: Geneva Street Food event (June): This gourmet event honors Geneva's unique food culture. Local and foreign food sellers congregate to provide a diverse selection of foods ranging from street food staples to gourmet inventions. This event is a must-see for foodies because of the live music, entertainment, and dynamic environment.

Please keep in mind that the dates and specifics of these festivals and events may change from year to year, so check the official websites or local event calendars for the most up-to-date information before arranging your visit to Geneva.

Top Cities To Stay in Geneva

Geneva is a lovely city in Switzerland recognized for its magnificent surroundings, rich history, and worldwide clout. While Geneva is a famous tourist destination, there are numerous adjacent towns that provide excellent lodging options for those touring the area. Here are some of the best cities to visit:

Lausanne is a bustling city with a young ambiance, located on the beaches of Lake Geneva. It is home to the International Olympic Committee and has a diverse range of historical sites, cultural attractions, and a vibrant nightlife.

Montreux: A lovely city located on the banks of Lake Geneva, Montreux is famous for its annual jazz festival. It has attractions such as Chillon Castle and the Freddie Mercury monument, as well as spectacular views of the lake and the neighboring Alps.

Nyon: A picturesque medieval town with a rich history, Nyon is located on the northern banks of Lake Geneva. Visitors may see the Nyon Castle, wander around the lovely Old Town, and take in the stunning lake vistas.

Yvoire: A medieval treasure on the beaches of Lake Geneva, Yvoire is another French town near Geneva. It's famous for its well-preserved medieval buildings, lovely gardens, and flower-filled alleys.

These locations feature a variety of lodgings, ranging from luxury hotels to budget-friendly alternatives, as well as easy access to Geneva and the surrounding regions. Whether you want to learn about history, go on outdoor adventures, or attend cultural events, these cities are great places to start your trip in the Geneva area.

Chapter Four

Historical Monuments And Art Galleries in Geneva

Geneva, Switzerland, is well-known for its long history and thriving art scene. Numerous historical structures and art galleries highlight the city's cultural legacy. The Jet d'Eau, a beautiful water fountain on Lake Geneva, is one of the city's most recognizable monuments. The tower of the St. Pierre Cathedral, a Gothic masterpiece, provides panoramic views. The Maison Tavel, Geneva's oldest residence, features a museum tracing the city's history. Art lovers may visit the Musée d'Art et d'Histoire, which has a large collection of art from many eras. The Patek Philippe Museum has excellent watches, while the Museum of Natural History houses amazing natural science exhibits. Visitors interested in contemporary art may go to the Museum of Modern and Contemporary Art, which features shows by both Swiss and foreign artists. Geneva, with its combination of history and cultural expression, provides tourists with an enthralling experience.

Geneva's Historitage and Cultural Monuments

Geneva, Switzerland, is a city rich in history and tradition, with several historical monuments demonstrating the city's cultural and architectural importance. Here are some of Geneva's famous heritage and historical monuments:

St. Pierre Cathedral: One of Geneva's most distinctive monuments, St. Pierre Cathedral is located in the center of the Old Town. This gorgeous church, which dates back to the 12th century, provides breathtaking views of the city from its towers. It is also historically significant since it was a focal point of John Calvin's Protestant Reformation.

The Jet d'Eau is a well-known water fountain situated on Lake Geneva. It blasts water up to 140 meters into the air and is one of the city's most identifiable icons. Despite its lack of historical significance, it has become a beloved element of Geneva's skyline since its construction in the nineteenth century.

The Reformation Wall is a monument situated in the Parc des Bastions. It is also known as the Wall of the Reformers. It honors the Protestant Reformation leaders with sculptures of famous personalities such as John Calvin, William Farel, Theodore Beza, and John Knox. The monument commemorates Geneva's pivotal role in the Reformation movement.

Maison Tavel: Dating from the 14th century, Maison Tavel is Geneva's oldest home. It is currently the Museum of Geneva History, providing tourists with an insight into the city's history. The museum shows relics, records, and interactive displays that tell the narrative of Geneva from its beginnings to the present.

Barbier-Mueller Museum: The Barbier-Mueller Museum is well-known for its collection of tribal and antique art. The museum is housed in a lovely estate on Lake Geneva and shows items from diverse civilizations such as Africa, Oceania, Asia, and the Americas. It provides visitors with a one-of-a-kind chance to learn about many cultures and civilizations via art and historical artifacts.

Geneva's Old Town, also known as Vieille Ville, is a picturesque district that highlights the city's ancient architecture and narrow cobblestone alleyways. Exploring the Old Town offers tourists the opportunity to explore ancient structures such as Maison Tavel as well as lovely squares such as Place du Bourg-de-Four, Geneva's oldest plaza.

These are only a handful of Geneva's numerous cultural and historical landmarks. The city has a rich history and allows tourists to dive into it while enjoying its dynamic current.

Contemporary Art Galleries And Museums

Geneva, Switzerland, has a thriving art scene including various modern art galleries and museums. Here are a few important ones to look into:

Genève Centre d'Art Contemporain: This contemporary art center exhibits cutting-edge works by established and upcoming artists. Exhibitions, performances, films, and other art-related activities are held here.

MAMCO (Musée d'Art Moderne et Contemporain): MAMCO is Geneva's foremost modern and contemporary art museum. It has an extensive collection of works dating from the 1960s to the present, including paintings, sculptures, installations, and multimedia art.

Galerie Eva Presenhuber: This gallery, located in the center of Geneva, represents a diverse spectrum of prominent contemporary artists, including Urs Fischer, John Armleder, and Doug Aitken. It conducts exhibits and art activities on a regular basis.

Xippas Galerie: Xippas is a modern art gallery with sites all over the globe, including Geneva. It displays modern artists' work in a variety of disciplines, including painting, sculpture, photography, and video art.

Analix Forever: Analix Forever, located in the heart of Geneva's art area, is a contemporary art gallery noted for its wide and unique shows. It showcases works by both renowned and upcoming artists.

Galerie Laurence Bernard specializes in contemporary art and exhibits works by worldwide artists in a variety of disciplines such as painting, photography, sculpture, and installation.

ArtLab Geneva: ArtLab Geneva is a fascinating museum that examines the convergence of art, science, and technology. Interactive installations, multimedia displays, and immersive experiences are included.

These are only a handful of Geneva's modern art galleries and institutions. Because the city has a diverse cultural environment, you may stumble across other galleries, pop-up exhibits, and art events throughout your stay.

National Parks and Reserves in Geneva

There are no national parks or reserves named after or in the vicinity of Geneva, Switzerland. Switzerland, on the other hand, has a number of national parks and protected areas spread around the country. Here are a few examples:

Swiss National Park: The Swiss National Park is the country's oldest national park, located in the canton of Graubünden. It has around 65 square kilometers of land area and is recognized for its rich alpine flora and wildlife.

Parc Jura Vaudois: The Parc Jura Vaudois is a regional nature park in the canton of Vaud that covers the Jura Mountains. It has stunning scenery, lush woods, and hiking routes.

Naturpark Thal: Naturpark Thal is a natural park in the canton of Solothurn that comprises the Thal valley and adjacent mountains. It is well-known for its diverse biodiversity as well as its cultural history.

Biosfera Val Müstair: This biosphere reserve is located in the canton of Graubünden, near the Italian border. It is known for its high alpine scenery, such as the Val Müstair valley and the Swiss National Park.

While these parks are not especially affiliated with Geneva, they represent examples of Switzerland's natural beauty and protected regions. Please keep in mind that developments or changes may have occurred after my previous update, so it's always a good idea to review up-to-date sources for the most accurate and current information.

Gardens And Romantic Couples Packs

There are various possibilities for romantic couples packs and gardens in Geneva that may improve your experience. Geneva, Switzerland, is well-known for its picturesque scenery and romantic atmosphere. Here are some ideas for romantic couples packages and gardens in Geneva:

Parc des Bastions: A gorgeous park in the center of Geneva, Parc des Bastions has lush foliage, tree-lined walks, and magnificent sculptures. It's ideal for a romantic walk or a picnic with your significant other.

Jardin Anglais: Located on the beaches of Lake Geneva, the Jardin Anglais (English Garden) provides breathtaking views of the lake as well as the Jet d'Eau, Geneva's famed water fountain. The park's bright flower beds, groomed lawns, and lovely walks provide a romantic atmosphere for couples.

Parc La Grange: Located on the right shore of Lake Geneva, this park is famous for its exquisite rose garden. It gives a beautiful backdrop for couples to explore and enjoy the fragrant blossoms with over 200 species of roses.

Villa Diodati: Villa Diodati, located on the banks of Lake Geneva in the commune of Cologny, is historically significant as the location where Mary Shelley penned her renowned work "Frankenstein." The grounds of the villa provide a calm and romantic setting, ideal for couples seeking a quiet and inspirational location.

Parc des Eaux-Vives: A delightful park with manicured gardens, fountains, and a wonderful view of Lake Geneva, Parc des Eaux-Vives is nestled between Lake Geneva and the Geneva Golf Club. It's a lovely spot for a romantic stroll, a picnic, or perhaps a candlelight supper at one of the park's restaurants.

When it comes to couples packs, Geneva has a variety of things to enjoy together. Consider taking a romantic boat excursion on Lake Geneva, walking around the lovely Old Town, visiting a spa for a couple's massage and relaxation, or perhaps going on a wine tasting tour in the neighboring vineyards.

Remember to double-check the most up-to-date information and opening hours for the gardens and parks, since they may change based on the season and local legislation.

Geneva Zoos and Educational Museums

There are various zoos and educational museums in Geneva that provide tourists with a range of experiences. Here are a few examples:

1: The Geneva Museum of Natural History (Muséum d'histoire naturelle de Genève) is a natural history museum with substantial displays on geology, paleontology, zoology, botany, and anthropology. Over 2 million specimens are on exhibit, including dinosaur fossils, animal dioramas, and interactive displays.

2: The Patek Philippe Museum exhibits the history of watchmaking and horology. It has an extensive collection of timepieces, such as antique watches, pocket watches, and intricate mechanical clocks. The exhibitions teach visitors about the art and science of watchmaking.

3: The Museum of Art and History (Musée d'Art et d'Histoire) exhibits a diverse collection of art and historical items. It houses several eras' collections of paintings, sculptures, pottery, textiles, and archaeological relics. Temporary exhibits on diverse topics are also held in the museum.

4: The Vivarium de Meyrin is a small-scale zoo specializing in reptiles and amphibians. It is home to a wide range of creatures, including snakes, lizards, turtles, and frogs. In their naturalistic settings, visitors may watch and learn about these interesting species.

5: The Natural History Museum of Geneva (Musée d'histoire naturelle de Genève) is a natural history museum that has exhibits on biodiversity, evolution, and ecosystems. It includes exhibits on local flora and animals, as well as worldwide biodiversity and environmental challenges.

These are only a handful of Geneva's zoos and educational museums. Each of these locations provides visitors of all ages with distinct educational opportunities. For the most up-to-date information on exhibitions, opening hours, and entry rates, always visit their websites or contact them directly.

Chapter Five

Eco-Friendly Accommodations in Geneva And Price Rates

Geneva Eco Friendly Accommodations is a popular choice for those looking for a peaceful and environmentally friendly escape. With a strong emphasis on comfort and relaxation, these hotels provide a broad variety of facilities aimed to improve their customers' well-being.

The spa facilities at Geneva Eco Friendly Accommodations are unrivaled, offering a haven for renewal and tranquility. Guests may enjoy a range of wellness experiences suited to their requirements, ranging from luxury massage therapies to reviving body treatments. The trained therapists utilize organic and ecologically safe materials to provide a comprehensive and environmentally responsible approach to relaxing.

Geneva Eco Friendly Accommodations provide a variety of social activities in addition to superb spa facilities. Guests may relax in wide social spaces, meet with other tourists, or participate in intriguing discussions. Social events and activities are often organized by the lodgings, building a feeling of community and developing meaningful relationships among visitors. Furthermore, these environmentally friendly lodgings stress sustainability in all parts of their business. Every effort is taken to reduce the carbon impact and assist the local community, from energy-efficient techniques to locally sourced organic food alternatives.

Finally, Geneva Eco Friendly Accommodations provide a well-balanced mix of comfort, spa amenities, relaxation, and social involvement. Guests may rest, recharge, and interact with like-minded folks while enjoying the beauty of their natural surroundings if they commit to sustainable behaviors.

Tourist Hotels & Resorts on a Budget

It's vital to remember that Geneva, Switzerland, is recognized for being an expensive city when it comes to budget-friendly hotels and resorts. In comparison to other places, lodging costs might be rather costly. However, there are still some solutions accessible with lower pricing. Here are a few hotels and resorts in Geneva that are reasonably priced:

Hotel ibis Genève Centre Nations: This hotel, located near the United Nations headquarters, provides modest and pleasant rooms at a moderate price. Prices begin at $100 per night.

Hotel ibis Genève Aéroport: Located near Geneva Airport, this hotel offers easy access to public transit. The rooms are simple but provide decent value for money. Prices start at about $100 per night.

Hotel Cornavin Genève: Located near Geneva's major railway station, this hotel is ideal for visiting the city. The rooms are clean and pleasant, with nightly prices beginning about $120.

Hotel Montana Geneva: This hotel, located near Lake Geneva, provides pleasant accommodations at reasonable prices. Prices start at about $130 per night.

Hotel Moderne: Located in the center of Geneva, this hotel is close to several attractions. The accommodations are basic but well-kept, with costs beginning about $140 per night.

Please keep in mind that these costs are estimates and may change based on the season and availability. To acquire the most up-to-date information and compare costs, always check with hotels directly or utilize online booking platforms.

PoLuxury Tourist Hotels & Resorts in Geneva

Here are several premium tourist hotels and resorts in Geneva, Switzerland, with approximate prices.

Four Seasons Hotel des Bergues Geneva: Located in the center of Geneva, this historic hotel offers luxury accommodations, superb dining choices, and a spa. Prices begin at $600 per night.

Hotel d'Angleterre: This beautiful hotel on the shores of Lake Geneva has sumptuous accommodations, a Michelin-starred restaurant, and spectacular lake views. Prices begin at $700 per night.

The Ritz-Carlton Hotel de la Paix, Geneva: This upmarket hotel has elegant accommodations, a rooftop bar, and is conveniently located near Lake Geneva. Prices begin about $550 per night.

Mandarin Oriental, Geneva: This magnificent hotel on the Rhône River has large rooms, a gourmet restaurant, and a beautiful spa. Prices begin at $600 per night.

Beau-Rivage Geneva: This distinguished hotel on the banks of Lake Geneva provides magnificent accommodations, a renowned restaurant, and a lakefront patio. Prices begin at $500 per night.

Grand Hotel Kempinski Geneva: This 5-star hotel offers elegant accommodations, a variety of dining choices, and a spa facility with spectacular city views. Prices begin at $400 per night.

Hotel President Wilson: This hotel provides magnificent rooms, exquisite restaurants, and a rooftop spa, as well as breathtaking views of Lake Geneva and Mont Blanc. Prices begin at $500 per night.

Please keep in mind that these are just estimates and might change depending on variables such as room type, time of booking, and availability. It is best to check the particular hotel's website or contact them directly for the most up-to-date price information.

Vacation Rentals and Apartments

Because Geneva has a high cost of living, rental costs in the city may be relatively exorbitant when compared to other areas. Apartment and vacation rental prices might vary based on criteria such as location, size, amenities, and length of time.

Apartments: Apartment rental costs in Geneva may vary greatly. According to my understanding, a one-bedroom apartment in the city center would cost between CHF 2,000 and CHF 3,500 per month. Prices may be somewhat cheaper in the city's outskirts or in adjacent communities.

Vacation Rentals: Apartments, condominiums, and homes are available for rent in Geneva. Vacation rental fees might vary depending on criteria such as location, size, and the amount of luxury or facilities given. Depending on the sort of property and its location, vacation rentals in Geneva may cost anywhere from CHF 100 to CHF 500 or more each night.

Geneva Hostels and Guesthouses

When it comes to lodging, Geneva has a variety of alternatives, including guesthouses and hostels, which are often less expensive than hotels.

Here are a few Geneva guesthouses and hostels, along with their projected costs:

Geneva Hostel: Geneva Hostel is a popular alternative for budget tourists, located near Lake Geneva and the city center. They provide dormitory-style rooms with common bathrooms. Prices range from $35 and $50 per night, depending on the season and accommodation type.

City Hostel Geneva: City Hostel Geneva offers economical accommodation near the major railway station and within walking distance of famous attractions. Dormitory beds with shared bathrooms are provided. Prices vary between $30 and $40 per night.

Nyon Hostel: Although not in Geneva, the Nyon Hostel is in the neighboring town of Nyon, which is readily accessible by rail from Geneva. The hostel has nice dorm rooms as well as individual rooms with shared utilities. Prices range between $30 and $40 per night.

Hotel St. Gervais: While it is a hotel, Hotel St. Gervais in Geneva has some affordable choices, such as single and double rooms with communal bathrooms. Depending on the accommodation type and season, prices normally vary from $80-$120 per night.

Les Armures Guesthouse: Les Armures Guest House is located in the heart of Geneva's Old Town and provides a pleasant and historic ambiance. The rooms at the guesthouse are uniquely designed and have private bathrooms. Prices vary, but often begin at $150-$200 per night.

Locations for Tourist Camps in Geneva

There are various campgrounds and campsites in Geneva, Switzerland, where travelers may stay. Here are some common choices:

Camping Indigo Genève: Located on the beaches of Lake Geneva, this campground provides a picturesque environment as well as a variety of services such as power connections, Wi-Fi, showers, and a restaurant. Prices vary according on season, kind of lodging (tent, caravan, or motorhome), and number of guests. On average, a basic pitch will cost between CHF 30 and CHF 40 each night.

Camping Bois de Bay: Located in a green location near the city center, Camping Bois de Bay provides tent, camper, and motorhome spaces. The campground has amenities such as power, showers, and laundry. The costs per night vary from CHF 20 to CHF 30 depending on the season and kind of lodging.

Camping La Colombière: Another popular alternative is Camping La Colombière, which is located in Versoix, a town near Geneva. It has a swimming pool, a restaurant, and a children's playground among its attractions. Prices for a basic pitch start at about CHF 25 per night.

Camping Vidy: Camping Vidy is located on the outskirts of Geneva, near Lake Geneva, and offers a convenient position with easy access to the city center. Showers, laundry, and a restaurant are available at the campground. Prices per night might vary from CHF 20 to CHF 30 depending on the season and kind of lodging.

Please keep in mind that the costs shown above are estimates and subject to change. It is always suggested to check the official websites or directly contact the campsites for the most up-to-date information on availability and fees based on the dates of your vacation.

Chapter Six

Geneva Nightlife At A Glance

Geneva has a dynamic and diversified nightlife that is likely to please any visitor. The city accommodates all interests and inclinations, from fashionable clubs to honey taverns. Visitors may enjoy live music, great beverages, or just take up the bustling environment while socializing with locals and other visitors. The city's well-known hospitality guarantees a warm welcome and unforgettable experiences. Geneva, with its magnificent lakeside location and a variety of entertainment alternatives, is the ideal venue for flexing and enjoying the night to the utmost. Geneva's nightlife provides something for everyone, whether you want a laid-back evening or an intense party atmosphere.

A Guide To Geneva City Bars and Nightclubs

Geneva, Switzerland, has a thriving nightlife culture with a wide range of busy pubs and nightclubs to satisfy all preferences. Geneva offers it all, whether you're searching for a contemporary cocktail bar, a vibrant dance club, or a place to unwind with live music. Here's a list of some of Geneva's most popular pubs and nightclubs:

Java Club: Java Club is a prominent nightclub in Geneva noted for its dynamic atmosphere and different music genres. The club offers both local and international DJs who play anything from house and techno to hip-hop and R&B. It's a terrific spot to spend the night dancing.

L'Usine is a multi-purpose arena that serves as a center for art, entertainment, and nightlife. L'Usine is home to many pubs, a performance theater, and a club. Here you may see live music performances, DJ sets, and themed events. The venue often features alternative and indie music, drawing a broad audience.

La Gravière is a unique nightclub and cultural place located in an industrial region. It presents underground electronic music events ranging from techno to house to experimental. The club features a relaxed ambiance and a spacious outside space that is ideal for summer evenings.

Barbershop: Barbershop is a must-visit if you're searching for a sophisticated martini bar. With a concealed entrance and an immaculate atmosphere, it offers a speakeasy feel.

The bar's broad drink menu features traditional and unique cocktails crafted by professional mixologists. The comfortable and refined ambience is great for personal chats.

Le Chat Noir: Le Chat Noir, which combines a bar, a restaurant, and a live music venue, provides a varied entertainment experience. The pub presents live acts on a regular basis, ranging from jazz and blues to rock and pop. Enjoy a wonderful lunch while sipping beverages and taking in the vibrant scene.

Mr. Pickwick Pub: Mr. Pickwick is a popular alternative for people looking for a British pub experience. This tavern, located near the Geneva railway station, serves a broad variety of beers, including British ales and other brews. You may watch live sports on giant screens, play billiards, and eat pub cuisine in a relaxed atmosphere.

Silencio Club: Inspired by David Lynch's film "Mulholland Drive," the Silencio Club adds a touch of exclusivity to Geneva's evening scene. It is a members-only club, however non-members may attend with a reservation. In an expensive and small environment, the facility hosts a combination of live concerts, DJ sets, and art exhibits.

Always double-check the opening hours, admittance restrictions, and event schedules before visiting any given place. Furthermore, the nightlife culture in Geneva may change, so research local resources or ask locals for advice. Have fun on your evenings out in Geneva!

How to Locate Live Music Venues and Jazz Clubs

Follow these methods to locate live music venues and jazz bars in Geneva:

1: Online Search: Use search engines such as Google, Yahoo, or Bing to do an online search. To discover relevant results, use keywords like "live music venues in Geneva" or "jazz bars in Geneva."

2: Investigate social media networks such as Facebook, Twitter, and Instagram. Many music establishments and pubs use these platforms to publicize their events and performances. To find suitable venues, look for hashtags such as #GenevaMusic or #JazzBarsGeneva.

3: Check out local event listings websites, both general and music-specific. Websites such as Eventbrite, Meetup, and

Songkick often highlight upcoming live music events and concerts in places such as Geneva.

4: City Guides: Look for city guides or online periodicals that specialize in the Geneva entertainment scene. These books often include curated listings of suggested music venues and pubs. Websites such as Time Out Geneva and Geneva Tourism may be valuable tools.

5: Interact with residents or expat communities in Geneva through forums, social media groups, or online communities. Based on their own experiences or knowledge of the local music scene, they may provide important suggestions.

6: Check with Hotels or Tourist Information Centers: If you're in Geneva, check with the concierge desk at your hotel or the local tourist information center. They can provide you printed information, maps, and recommendations for live music venues and jazz pubs throughout the city.

7: Attend Local Festivals or Events: Keep an eye out for local festivals or events with live music performances. These concerts often bring together a variety of artists and performers and may be a fantastic opportunity to find new venues and explore the Geneva music scene.

Jazz And Live Music Venues

Geneva, Switzerland, has a thriving live music scene with a variety of venues catering to many genres, including jazz. Here are some of Geneva's most popular live music and jazz venues:

AMR - Association for the Promotion of Improvised Music: AMR, located in the Quartier des Grottes, is a well-known jazz and improvisational music venue. It presents frequent performances by local and international jazz musicians.

Chat Noir: Chat Noir is a traditional cabaret-style venue in the center of Geneva recognized for its diversified music program. It often includes jazz performances, as well as blues and world music.

La Gravière: This underground music club features a diverse spectrum of genres such as jazz, experimental music, and electronic music. Regular concerts and DJ sets are held at La Gravière, providing a lively and alternative ambiance.

Le Caveau de la Huchette: Although not in Geneva, the adjacent Parisian restaurant Le Caveau de la Huchette is worth noting. It is a famed jazz club that has featured some of the best jazz performers since 1946. It's a memorable experience if you're willing to take a short journey to Paris.

Temple de la Madeleine: This lovely ancient cathedral hosts jazz concerts and other musical activities on occasion. It has a one-of-a-kind environment and superb acoustics for listening to live music.

While there is no fixed site, the Django Reinhardt Jazz Festival is an annual event conducted in June at several places in and around Geneva. It honors the legendary jazz guitarist Django Reinhardt through performances, jam sessions, and seminars.

These are only a few examples of Geneva's live music and jazz venues. It's always a good idea to check their schedules or search local listings to learn about the most recent performances and activities in town.

Tips For Having a Memorable Night In Geneva

If you want to make the most of your nighttime experience in Geneva, here are some suggestions:

Explore Geneva's Old Town: Geneva's Old Town is recognized for its picturesque lanes lined with taverns, clubs, and restaurants. Take a walk along the small alleyways to find hidden jewels that provide unique nighttime experiences.

Visit the Rive Gauche: The Rive Gauche is a bustling area of Geneva situated on the Rhône River's left bank. It's teeming with hip pubs, clubs, and live music venues. Check out the Eaux-Vives and Pâquis areas, which are quite busy at night.

Take advantage of Lake Geneva's magnificent lakefront location. Many restaurants and clubs have lakeside terraces where you may sip cocktails while taking in the scenery. During the summer, some establishments even host boat parties or floating bars.

Attend Live Music Events: Geneva boasts a vibrant music scene with a wide range of venues holding live performances. Check the local listings for upcoming concerts, jazz clubs, and other music events.

Experience the International Scene: Geneva is a global city that is home to many expatriates and organizations. Visit pubs or clubs that attract individuals from all backgrounds and cultures to meet people from diverse backgrounds and cultures.

Try Swiss Specialties: Switzerland is well-known for its delectable beverages and cuisine. Swiss delicacies such as absinthe, local wines, and fondue may improve your evening experience while also providing a distinct cultural experience.

Make Reservations: Popular nightlife locations in Geneva may fill up quickly, particularly on weekends. Reservations are recommended, particularly for restaurants and elite clubs, to guarantee you have a place and prevent excessive wait periods.

Dress standards: Some Geneva clubs and upmarket businesses have stringent dress standards. To guarantee seamless access, dress tastefully and suitably for the event you want to attend.

Consider Public Transportation: Geneva has a well-developed public transportation system that includes buses, trams, and trains. Consider using public transit at night to move about the city since parking might be scarce and pricey in certain regions.

Maintain Your Safety: As with any evening event, it is critical to prioritize your safety. Keep to well-lit locations, travel with companions whenever feasible, and keep an eye on your valuables. If you're unfamiliar with the city, try asking residents or hotel employees for ideas and safety advice.

Remember that everyone's concept of a great nighttime experience is different, so feel free to modify these suggestions to your tastes. Have a great day discovering Geneva's bustling nightlife!

Chapter Seven

Shopping And Dining Etiquette in Geneva

Geneva, Switzerland, provides a gastronomic experience that entices the taste senses with its sweet and delectable tastes. The city has a great dessert culture, with everything from decadent Swiss chocolates to beautiful pastries. Traditional Swiss sweets, such as Toblerone mousse, Swiss chocolate fondue, and creamy Meringue with Gruyère double cream, are divine. The city is also well-known for its velvety smooth hot chocolate made from the best Swiss chocolate. Geneva has a selection of delicious sorbets and handmade ice creams for a refreshing treat. To go with these wonderful delicacies, the city has a selection of outstanding Swiss wines noted for their remarkable quality and complexity. Geneva, with its attention to cuisine, perfectly embodies the sense of sweet pleasure, making it a food and drink enthusiast's delight.

Favorite Geneva Food And Cuisines

Geneva, Switzerland's second-most populated city, is noted for its diversified culinary culture. Here are some of Geneva's favorite dishes and cuisines:

Geneva provides a broad variety of classic Swiss meals. Fondue is a popular Swiss meal that consists of melted cheese eaten with bread, potatoes, and pickles. Another popular meal is raclette, which includes melting cheese and scraping it into boiling potatoes with pickles and onions. Rösti, a crispy potato pancake, is another popular Swiss dish.

1: French Cuisine: Because Geneva is situated on the French border, French cuisine has a strong effect on the local culinary culture. Many restaurants serve classic French cuisine such as Coq au Vin (chicken cooked in red wine), Escargots de Bourgogne (snails in garlic butter), and Ratatouille (vegetable stew).

2; Mediterranean Cuisine: Geneva's gastronomic choices reflect its closeness to Italy and the Mediterranean. Pasta, wood-fired pizza, fresh seafood, and flavorful Mediterranean salads are popular throughout the city.

3: Geneva has a varied spectrum of foreign cuisines as a result of its cosmopolitan population. Restaurants provide meals from all over the globe, including Chinese, Thai, Indian, Japanese, Mexican, and Middle Eastern fare. This type enables both residents and tourists to sample a broad range of tastes.

4: Chocolate and pastries: Geneva, like the rest of Switzerland, is famous for its chocolate. Swiss chocolates, like Toblerone and Lindt, are readily accessible, and there are other artisanal chocolatiers around the city. Geneva also boasts a strong pastry culture, with various patisseries serving delectable pastries, cakes, and sweets.

5: Swiss Cheese: Switzerland is famed for its cheese, and Geneva provides an opportunity to sample a variety of Swiss cheese kinds. Along with fondue and raclette, you can discover Gruyère, Emmental, Appenzeller, and a variety of other delectable Swiss cheeses.

Overall, Geneva offers a gastronomic experience that blends Swiss, French, Mediterranean, and international cuisines, making it a foodie's dream.

Favorite Drinks in Geneva

Depending on your interests, you may enjoy a variety of popular beverages in Geneva. Here are several possibilities:

Swiss Wine: Switzerland is well-known for producing high-quality wines, and Geneva is no exception. Local Swiss wines such as Chasselas, Pinot Noir, and Gamay are available. Geneva is also adjacent to the well-known wine districts of Valais and Vaud, where a greater range of Swiss wines may be found.

Swiss Beer: Switzerland has a thriving craft beer culture, with local brewers in Geneva producing a variety of innovative and tasty brews. Lagers, ales, and wheat beers are popular beer genres in Switzerland.

Absinthe has ancient origins in Switzerland, notably in the French-speaking area of Geneva. While it was forbidden for many years, it has made a resurgence, and absinthe establishments can again be found in Geneva. Enjoy it with water and sugar, or experiment with newer variants of this anise-flavored spirit.

Cocktails: Geneva boasts a thriving cocktail culture, with several pubs and lounges serving up inventive and well-crafted concoctions. You may sample traditional drinks as well as new concoctions produced by professional bartenders.

Hot Chocolate: Geneva, like the rest of Switzerland, is famed for its rich and velvety hot chocolate. Indulging in a cup of Swiss hot chocolate may be a lovely experience, whether you're traveling during the winter months or just want a comfortable treat.

It's crucial to remember that everyone's tastes are different, and these ideas are simply a starting point. When in Geneva, explore the local cafés, pubs, and restaurants to find your own favorite beverages depending on your taste preferences.

Vegetarians and Vegans Options in Geneva

Geneva, Switzerland has a number of vegetarian and vegan restaurants. Here are some prominent vegetarian and vegan restaurants in Geneva:

VegiTerranean: This restaurant specializes in vegetarian and vegan food, with a menu full of dishes influenced by Mediterranean and world cuisines.

Tibits is a vegetarian and vegan buffet-style restaurant featuring a variety of selections such as salads, soups, hot meals, and desserts. You pay by weight, which allows you to personalize your meal.

Veganopolis: This vegan restaurant in Geneva offers a wide range of plant-based cuisine, including burgers, sandwiches, bowls, and desserts. They emphasize the use of fresh, organic foods.

Holy Cow! is a vegetarian restaurant that serves a range of world cuisines such as Indian, Mexican, and Mediterranean. They also feature a variety of vegan alternatives.

Le Point G: Known for its delectable pastries, cakes, and sweets, this vegan-friendly bakery and café in Geneva. Vegan sandwiches and salads are also available.

Hüsi Bierhaus: While not entirely vegetarian or vegan, this quaint bar provides a variety of plant-based alternatives, including vegan burgers, salads, and soups. They also offer a wide variety of vegan beers.

Herbivore Vegan Shop and Café: Herbivore is a vegan shop with a café located in the center of Geneva. They sell a variety of vegan goods such as food, cosmetics, and home stuff. While perusing, you may have a vegan snack or drink.

Carouge Food Market: This market is held every Wednesday and Saturday in Carouge, a Geneva neighborhood. A variety of merchants provide fresh produce, handcrafted goods, and vegetarian and vegan cuisine alternatives.

These are only a few examples of vegetarian and vegan restaurants in Geneva. Many other eateries in the city also cater to plant-based diets, so you should have no trouble finding acceptable selections. Check the hours of operation and make reservations if necessary, particularly for popular establishments.

Best Cafes & Restaurants in Geneva

Geneva is recognized for its bustling culinary scene, which includes a diverse selection of cafés and restaurants to satisfy every taste. Here are some of Geneva's greatest cafés and restaurants:

Café du Centre: This beautiful café in the center of Geneva provides delectable pastries, sandwiches, and a choice of hot and cold drinks. It's a nice location to unwind and have a cup of coffee.

Chez ma Cousine: This popular eatery delivers substantial servings of rotisserie chicken at reasonable pricing. The comfortable ambiance and good service make it a local and tourist favorite.

Café des Bains: Located in the fashionable Plainpalais district, Café des Bains is a chic café recognized for its creative environment and wonderful cuisine. They include a wide range of vegetarian and vegan meals, as well as a large selection of beverages.

Café du Soleil: One of Geneva's oldest cafés, Café du Soleil was founded in 1705. It offers a genuine Swiss ambience and serves traditional Swiss fare including fondue and raclette. The outside patio is ideal for taking advantage of the nice weather.

Les Armures: This upmarket restaurant is recognized for its sophisticated Swiss cuisine and is housed in a historic structure. Fondue, rösti, and gourmet meat specialities are among the items on the menu. It is great for special events because of its exquisite atmosphere and professional service.

Cottage Café: A quiet café with wonderful food and a comfortable environment. Salads, sandwiches, quiches, and desserts are among the handmade meals available. During the summer, the outside sitting area is quite beautiful.

Café du Marché: Located in the old town, this café is a local favorite for its delicious pastries and outstanding coffee. The pleasant decor and helpful personnel provide for a comfortable setting for a quick snack or a leisurely supper.

Buvette des Bains: Located on the beaches of Lake Geneva, Buvette des Bains provides breathtaking views and a relaxed environment. It's a lovely area for a refreshing drink or a bite to eat while admiring the environment.

These are just a handful of the many excellent cafés and restaurants in Geneva. Whether you like traditional Swiss cuisine or foreign dishes, Geneva offers something for everyone.

Geneva Dining Etiquette

Geneva, Switzerland's cosmopolitan capital, has its own set of dining etiquette and traditions. Here are some rules to follow while eating in Geneva:

- Punctuality: It is considered courteous in Geneva to appear on time for a meal reservation. Because the Swiss appreciate timeliness, it is essential to avoid being late.

- Table Manners: Wait to be seated at a dinner table or follow the host's directions. Keep your hands but not your elbows on the table. Do not begin eating until the host or the most senior member of the table does.

- Cutlery Usage: The Swiss eat in the European way, with the fork in the left hand and the knife in the right, when cutting food. After cutting, set the knife on the plate's edge, blade facing inward. Rather than eating with your hands, it is courteous to use silverware throughout the meal.

- Bread Etiquette: When eating bread, it is normal to break off a piece and consume it rather than bite right into the loaf. Instead of placing the bread immediately on the table, place it on your plate.

- Wine and toasts: Switzerland is well-known for its wine, and it is customary to offer wine with meals. When toasting, establish eye contact with the person toasting and softly clink glasses. Crossing one's arms when toasting is considered disrespectful.

- Tipping: Service costs are usually included in the bill in Geneva. However, if you are pleased with the service, it is customary to offer a little tip. A 5-10% gratuity is welcomed but not required.

- During the dinner, engage in polite conversation but avoid sensitive issues such as politics or religion.

Because Swiss people cherish their privacy, it is better to avoid asking personal inquiries.

- Finishing the Meal: After you've completed your meal, arrange your cutlery on your plate parallel to each other, with the handles at 4 o'clock. This tells the waiter that you've completed your meal.

Remember that these are basic rules, and it's always a good idea to watch and follow the conduct of others around you. Respecting local traditions and etiquette will make your dining experience in Geneva more enjoyable.

Chapter Eight

What To Know Before Visiting Geneva As A First Time Visitor

Knowing the key recommendations before visiting Geneva is critical for a pleasant trip. Learn about local traditions, transit alternatives, currency exchange rates, famous tourist destinations, and the weather. Investigating these details promotes a more pleasurable and well-planned visit.

About Geneva currency

Geneva, Switzerland's second-most populated city, is well-known as a worldwide center for banking, diplomacy, and international organizations. The Swiss franc (CHF) is the currency used in Geneva and across Switzerland. The Swiss franc, which was introduced in 1798, is known for its stability and is commonly considered as a safe haven currency. It is measured in centimeters. The design of the money includes iconic Swiss symbols such as the Swiss coat of arms, Alpine scenery, and famous people. Geneva's financial industry, which includes private banking and wealth management, draws people and firms from all over the globe, making the Swiss franc a valuable currency for international transactions in the city.

Where Can I Exchange Money In Geneva?

There are many venues in Geneva, Switzerland, where you may exchange money. Here are some typical alternatives:

Banks: Currency exchange services are provided by banks in Geneva. You may exchange money at local branches of large Swiss banks such as UBS, Credit Suisse, or Banque Cantonale de Genève. They often provide reasonable rates, however take in mind that transaction costs may apply.

Exchange Offices: Several exchange offices, also known as bureaux de change, are found across Geneva. They often provide cheaper rates and may have extended working hours than banks. To assure dependability, look for approved exchange offices that carry the "Authorized Money Changer" symbol.

Swiss Post (La Poste) offices in Geneva also provide currency exchange services. They usually have acceptable conversion rates, and some bigger post offices may have specialized currency exchange desks.

Airports and railway Stations: Currency exchange counters are available at Geneva International Airport and the major railway station, Gare de Genève-Cornavin. Keep in mind, however, that certain places may have slightly higher costs or less attractive rates than other possibilities.

Hotels: Some Geneva hotels may provide currency exchange services to their visitors. However, hotel costs are often less cheap when compared to banks or exchange offices, so it's best to look into other choices first.

It's usually a good idea to examine rates and fees before transferring money to guarantee you receive the best bargain. Consider transferring bigger sums at once to save transaction expenses.

Consider Travel Insurance

It is a good idea to consider travel insurance while visiting Geneva. Travel insurance may offer you financial security and peace of mind in the event of an unforeseen circumstance or emergency during your vacation. Here are a few reasons why you might think about getting travel insurance for your trip to Geneva:

Medical Emergencies: Travel insurance may cover medical expenditures if you are injured or get unwell while on vacation. It may include coverage for doctor visits, hospitalization, prescriptions, and, if necessary, emergency medical evacuation.

Vacation Cancellation or Interruption: If you have to cancel or cut short your vacation due to unexpected circumstances such as sickness, injury, or family emergency, travel insurance may pay you for prepaid and non-refundable charges.

Lost or Delayed Baggage: If your baggage is lost, damaged, or delayed while traveling, travel insurance may cover the cost of replacing critical things or compensating you for the inconvenience.

Personal Liability: Travel insurance may include personal liability coverage, which protects you if you cause property damage or harm someone while on vacation.

Emergency support: Many travel insurance packages include 24-hour emergency support. Medical referrals, emergency financial transfers, translation assistance, and other travel-related issues may all be handled by these services.

It's critical to thoroughly research the coverage and policy specifics of any travel insurance plan you're thinking about getting. Insurance companies provide varying levels of coverage and may have particular exclusions or limits. Before making a choice, study the policy papers and understand what is and is not covered.

Remember that travel insurance should preferably be acquired prior to your trip to guarantee you have coverage from the outset.

LGBTQ + Acceptance

Geneva, Switzerland, is well-known for its progressive and open attitude toward the LGBTQ+ population. The city values diversity and advocates for LGBTQ+ rights, establishing an accepting atmosphere. The municipal government actively promotes LGBTQ+ rights projects, including as anti-discrimination legislation and equal marriage rights. In Geneva, LGBTQ+ groups flourish, giving vital support and services to the community. Pride activities and parades are publicly celebrated, drawing individuals from all areas of life. The city's bustling social scene includes LGBTQ+-friendly locations, clubs, and pubs where people may openly express themselves. The city of Geneva's dedication to LGBTQ+ acceptance is mirrored in its educational institutions, businesses, and healthcare facilities, all of which stress diversity and give complete assistance. The city's tolerance and commitment to equality contribute to a friendly climate in which LGBTQ+ people and their supporters may feel protected, respected, and cherished.

Emergency Contacts

In the event of an emergency in Geneva, Switzerland, dial the following emergency numbers:

117 police officers
The police emergency line is used to report crimes, emergencies, and to request law enforcement help.

144 ambulances

The ambulance emergency number is used to request medical help in the event of a medical emergency or accident.

118th Fire Department
Fires, rescue operations, and other fire-related situations are reported using the fire department emergency number.

General European Emergency Number: 112
The emergency number 112 may be phoned from any mobile or landline phone in Europe to contact emergency services such as police, ambulances, and fire departments.

Please keep in mind that these emergency contact numbers are just for Geneva, Switzerland. The emergency contact numbers may change depending on where you are. When visiting a new place, it is usually a good idea to get acquainted with the local emergency contact numbers.

Geneva Cultural Etiquette

As a multinational city and worldwide diplomatic hub, Geneva has its own cultural etiquette that inhabitants and tourists are required to follow. When it comes to cultural etiquette in Geneva, here are some fundamental standards to remember:

- Punctuality: In Geneva, being on time is highly respected. It's important to be on time, or even a few minutes early, whether you're attending a business meeting, a social gathering, or a cultural event.

- Greetings: When meeting someone for the first time, the most popular form of greeting in Geneva is a handshake. Maintain eye contact and smile when you welcome the individual. In more formal circumstances, people are addressed by their last names, followed by "Monsieur" or "Madame."

- Geneva is noted for its stylish and refined fashion sense. When attending formal events such as business meetings or cultural performances, dress conservatively and stylishly. However, in informal or outdoor situations, the dress code might be more lenient.

- Geneva is a bilingual city, with French being the major language. However, English, as well as other languages such as German and Italian, is frequently spoken. It is customary to greet individuals in French with "Bonjour" or "Bonsoir" (good morning or evening) before switching to English if required.

- Dining etiquette: Table manners are essential while eating in Geneva. Wait for the host to begin eating before you begin, and always keep your hands visible on the table. It is also usual to utilize utensils rather than eating with your hands, unless the item being served calls for it.

- Respect for personal space: Personal space and privacy are highly valued in Swiss society. It is critical to keep a proper distance from people, particularly while conversing. Unless you have a deep personal connection with someone, avoid touching them.

- Tipping is not as customary in Switzerland as it is in other countries since service costs are often included in the bill. However, a little gratuity for great service is appreciated. Before determining whether to give an extra tip, check the bill or inquire whether a service fee has already been included.

- Respect for local traditions and laws: Geneva is well-known for following rules and regulations. Respect for local norms, regulations, and cultural sensitivity is crucial. For example, smoking is not permitted in public areas, and it is courteous to get permission before photographing persons or specified sites.

These recommendations should help you manage Geneva's cultural etiquette. However, bear in mind that Geneva is a varied city with varying habits and expectations. To maintain courteous relationships, it's always a good idea to watch and follow the example of the locals.

Chapter Nine

Geneva Sustainable Budget Travel

Financial management and preparation are essential for a sustainable tourist experience in Geneva. Effective financial management ensures that you maximize your money and resources, enabling you to thoroughly explore and enjoy the city's attractions and experiences. You may manage finances for housing, transportation, food, and activities in a sustainable way by preparing a well-thought-out financial plan. This strategy allows you to support local companies while also reducing excessive spending, benefiting the city's economy and environment. Furthermore, financial planning may assist you in identifying possible cost-cutting alternatives, such as using public transportation or choosing economical but genuine local activities. You may improve your trip experience while also encouraging sustainability and ethical tourism in Geneva by adopting financial management and preparation.

Top Money Saving Strategies

Geneva is notorious for its high cost of living, but it is feasible to save money when living or traveling there with some careful preparation and wise decisions. Here are some of the best ways to save money in Geneva:

Use public transit: Geneva has a fantastic public transportation system that includes buses, trams, and trains. Using these choices instead of taxis or renting a vehicle may save you a lot of money on transportation costs.

Get a Geneva Transport Card: If you stay in a Geneva hotel, you may be eligible for a free Geneva Transport Card. This card allows you to use public transit throughout the city for the length of your stay, saving you money on individual prices.

Dine strategically: Eating out in Geneva may be costly, but there are methods to save costs. Look for lunch specials and fixed-price menus at restaurants, which are sometimes less expensive than supper selections. Consider visiting local markets and grocery shops for fresh vegetables and snacks, which may be less expensive than eating out every meal.

Discover free attractions: Geneva boasts a number of free attractions and activities that enable you to explore the city without paying any money. Visit gorgeous parks, walk along Lake Geneva, explore Old Town, or enjoy free museums and exhibits like the Maison Tavel or the Natural History Museum.

Take advantage of free events: Look for free events, concerts, and festivals in Geneva. Outdoor concerts and shows, especially during the summer months, are often available for free amusement.

Local markets: There are various local markets in Geneva where you may purchase fresh fruit, cheeses, bread, and other things at lower rates than supermarkets. Plainpalais Market and Carouge Market are famous places to visit.

Consider purchasing a Geneva Pass: If you want to visit many sites and museums, the Geneva Pass might be a good deal. It provides free or cheap admission to a variety of activities, including museums, boat trips, and guided tours. Examine your schedule to evaluate whether the pass fits your goals and budget.

Save money on lodging: Accommodation in Geneva may be expensive. Consider vacation rentals or hostels as alternatives to typical hotels, which may frequently provide more economical choices. Furthermore, booking ahead of time or during off-peak seasons may result in reduced prices.

Be aware of your water and power consumption: Utility expenses may quickly mount up, so be aware of your water and electricity usage. To help minimize your expenses, turn off lights when not in use, unplug gadgets when not in use, and use water wisely.

Examine for discounts and special deals offered to students, elderly, or certain memberships or loyalty programs. These discounts may be used for a variety of services, activities, and even transportation.

Remember that conserving money involves forethought and deliberate decisions. By following these guidelines and being cautious of your spending, you can make your stay in Geneva more cost-effective while still enjoying all the city has to offer.

Bargaining and Negotiation Strategies

Here are some pointers to remember while haggling and negotiating with market vendors in Geneva, Switzerland:

1: Do your homework: Before you go shopping, look into the normal price range for the item you want to buy. This will provide you with a starting point for talks and save you from overpaying.

2: Begin with a friendly tone: Begin the discussion with a cheerful and courteous manner. Developing a good connection with the seller might help you negotiate a mutually advantageous deal.

3: Active listening entails paying close attention to the seller's original price and any counteroffers they provide. This demonstrates respect and helps you to grasp their point of view, which may be useful in finding common ground.

4: Be self-assured and patient: Bargaining is prevalent in many marketplaces, so don't be scared to bargain. Maintain your confidence and patience during the process, since reaching an agreement that is satisfactory to all sides may take some time.

5: Use nonverbal cues: Body language may be very important in negotiations. Maintain eye contact, utilize hand gestures to convey curiosity or hesitancy, and watch your tone of speech. These nonverbal clues might aid in communicating your viewpoint and goals.

6: Start with a counteroffer that is somewhat lower than your ideal price but still within a fair range. This gives the seller flexibility to negotiate while also providing you an opportunity to get a good deal.

7: Highlight the seller's benefits: When making a counteroffer, underline any benefits or new business you can bring to the seller. Mention the prospect of future referrals or the purchase of numerous things, for example.

8: Prepare to walk away: If the seller refuses to meet your targeted price or the discussion fails to advance, be prepared to walk away. This might often cause the seller to rethink their stance and perhaps offer a better bargain.

9: Consider package deals: If you want to purchase many things from the same supplier, try to negotiate a package bargain. Bundling things together may sometimes result in lower costs.

10: Prepare a maximum budget: Keep your maximum budget in mind while bargaining. Don't let the haggling process get the better of you and wind up paying more than you anticipated.

Remember that negotiating is a cultural tradition in certain but not all marketplaces. While it may be widespread in certain sections of Geneva, it may not be as frequent in other markets. Respect local conventions and standards, and always participate in fair and respectful conversations.

Top Geneva Markets For Budget Shopping

There are various budget-friendly markets in Geneva, Switzerland, where you may discover a range of items and vegetables at low costs. Here are some of the most important budget marketplaces in Geneva:

Plainpalais Flea Market: This flea market is held every Wednesday and Saturday in the Plainpalais area. At reasonable costs, you may discover a large variety of used products, antiques, vintage clothes, books, and other stuff.

Les Grottes Market: This market, held every Thursday, provides a lively environment as well as a variety of fresh fruits, vegetables, cheeses, bread, and other local items. It's an excellent source of low-cost components for your meals.

Marché de Rive: Located on the shores of Lake Geneva, Marché de Rive is a famous food market that sells fresh vegetables, local items, flowers, and even street cuisine. It's a terrific place to go exploring and get low-cost, high-quality foods.

Carouge Market: This market is held on Wednesdays and Saturdays in the picturesque neighborhood of Carouge. You may shop for fruits, vegetables, flowers, cheese, meat, and other items at inexpensive costs.

Ferney-Voltaire Market: While officially outside Geneva, this market is located in the adjacent French town of Ferney-Voltaire. It is open on Saturdays and sells a variety of things at low costs, including fresh food, apparel, accessories, and home items.

These markets are well-known for offering a wide range of items at reasonable prices, enabling tourists to have a cost-effective shopping experience in Geneva. However, comparing pricing and exploring other booths to locate the greatest offers is always a smart idea.

Chapter Ten

Goodbye, Geneva

Leaving Geneva as a visitor is like saying goodbye to a tranquil dream. The city's breathtaking splendor, located between beautiful mountains and a glistening lake, leaves indelible memories.

A Guide To Favorite Geneva Swiss Souvenirs

When visiting Geneva, there are a number of popular tourist souvenirs to consider taking home. Here are a few of our favorites:

Swiss Chocolate: Switzerland is well-known for its delectable chocolate, and Geneva is home to a plethora of chocolatiers selling high-quality Swiss chocolate. For a sweet and tasty keepsake, look for well-known brands such as Toblerone, Lindt, or local artisanal chocolatiers.

Swiss Watches: Because Geneva is known as the world's watchmaking center, a Swiss watch is an exquisite and enduring keepsake. There are many different types of watches to pick from, ranging from premium brands like Rolex and Patek Philippe to more cheap ones.

Victorinox and Wenger, two famous Swiss Army Knife makers, have their origins in Switzerland. These flexible pocket knives are functional and well-crafted, making them a favorite tourist memento.

CERN Memorabilia: If you're interested in science and particle physics, the CERN gift store has CERN (European Organization for Nuclear Research) memorabilia. You may take a piece of cutting-edge research home with you by purchasing T-shirts, mugs, and other scientific-themed souvenirs.

Swiss Cheese: Switzerland is famed for its cheese, and Geneva has a wide selection of delectable cheeses. Popular cheeses include Gruyère, Emmental, and Appenzeller. As a pleasant and genuine keepsake, consider purchasing a variety of Swiss cheese.

Superb wine: Geneva is located in the center of Switzerland's wine region, which produces superb wines.

Look for local wines like Gamay, Pinot Noir, or Chasselas for a one-of-a-kind and delicious keepsake.

Fondue is a typical Swiss cuisine, and taking a fondue set back enables you to replicate the experience at home. Look for a package that contains a fondue pot, fondue forks, and all of the other fondue accessories.

Geneva-themed Souvenirs: Several souvenir stores in Geneva sell products that are uniquely tied to the city. Look for postcards, keychains, magnets, or ornamental goods with images of famous locations like the Jet d'Eau, St. Pierre Cathedral, or the Flower Clock.

Before buying souvenirs, remember to verify any customs requirements and limits on food or other things.

Safety Tips For First-Time Visitors

If you're a first-time visitor to Geneva, it's important to prioritize your safety and be cautious of your surroundings. While Geneva is typically a secure city, it is always a good idea to take measures to guarantee a pleasant and memorable vacation. Here are some safety considerations for first-time Geneva visitors:

Maintain vigilance in public locations: As in any big city, it is critical to maintain vigilance in public spaces, especially congested areas and tourist sites. Keep a watch on your stuff, particularly in congested areas such as railway stations, marketplaces, and famous tourist spots.

Use dependable transportation: Geneva has an extensive public transit system that includes buses, trams, and trains. Use these methods to avoid wandering alone in new regions, particularly at night. Taxis are another safe means of transportation; however, be sure they are licensed and utilize legitimate taxi stations.

Be wary of pickpockets: Pickpocketing may happen in busy places, so keep an eye on your things. Carry your handbag, wallet, or backpack close to your body and shut it using zippers or locks. Carry small quantities of cash and store critical papers, such as passports, in a hotel safe.

Respect local laws and customs: Become acquainted with Geneva's local laws and traditions. Switzerland has strong laws regulating drugs, public intoxication, and other behaviors. Always follow traffic laws, cross at appropriate crossings, and be conscious of local traditions and manners.

Protect your personal things: Never leave your goods unattended in public settings, such as a restaurant, café, or park. Maintain the security of your phone, camera, and other valuables, and avoid flashing costly goods that may draw unwanted attention.

At night, stay in well-lit and populous locations: While Geneva is typically safe at night, it's best to stay in well-lit and populated areas. Avoid going alone in poorly lit or remote places, and instead consider using public transit or hiring a trustworthy taxi service.

Be wary of scams: Scams may occur in every tourist site. Be aware of anyone who offers you unwanted assistance or attempts to distract you. Use trustworthy currency exchange agencies or ATMs for exchanging money.

Save Emergency contacts: vital phone numbers before your journey, such as local emergency services (such as police, ambulance, and fire department), your embassy or consulate, and the contact information for your lodging. Learn about the emergency protocols in your area.

Trust your instincts: If anything or someone makes you feel uneasy or suspicious, follow your instincts and leave the situation. Your safety is vital, so proceed with caution.

Have a wonderful day in this lovely city and travel safely!!!

Helpful Websites And Booking Resource

There are various platforms you may use to uncover useful websites and booking tools in Geneva, Switzerland. Here are a few of the best options:

Geneva tourist (official website): The official tourist website of Geneva gives detailed information about the city's attractions, events, lodging, and activities. You can discover guides, maps, and itineraries to help you organize your journey. *www.geneve.com* is the company's website.

Booking.com: A prominent online lodging booking site, Booking.com provides a broad choice of alternatives in Geneva, including hotels, flats, and guesthouses. You may narrow down your search by price, location, and guest reviews. Booking.com's website address is: *www.booking.com.*

Airbnb: If you want to stay in a private house or apartment, Airbnb is a great option. It enables you to rent directly from local hosts in Geneva. Depending on your interests and budget, you may choose from a variety of possibilities. AirBnB's website address is *www.airbnb.com.*

Expedia: Expedia is another well-known online travel firm that provides a variety of services, including airline and hotel reservations. In Geneva, you can get discounts and compare costs for lodging. Expedia's website address is *www.expedia.com.*

TripAdvisor is a website where travelers can obtain reviews, suggestions, and ratings for hotels, restaurants, and activities. You may make educated selections regarding your stay in Geneva by reading customer reviews. Visit the website at *www.tripadvisor.com.*

Geneva Airport: If you're traveling into Geneva, the official website of Geneva Airport provides important information on flights, transit alternatives, car rentals, and airport services. *www.gva.ch* is the website.

TPG (Geneva Public Transport): The TPG website offers information on public transportation in Geneva, such as buses, trams, and trains. To conveniently travel the city, you may obtain timetables, maps, and ticket information. *www.tpg.ch* is the website.

The Geneva Pass is a municipal pass that provides free entrance to a variety of attractions, museums, and public transit. You may save money by purchasing the pass online and exploring the city. Website: *http://www.geneva.com/en/see-do/geneva-pass/*

These websites and resources should assist you in planning your trip to Geneva, whether you're seeking lodging, transportation, or information on the city's attractions and services.

7 Days Itinerary In Geneva

Here's a 7-day schedule for every one who wishes to explore the best of Geneva while traveling on a budget in the morning, afternoon, and nighttime.

Day 1

Morning: Begin your day with a visit to the famed Jet d'Eau water fountain on Lake Geneva. It's an excellent location for taking photographs and admiring the breathtaking scenery. (Free)

Wander through the lovely small lanes of the Old Town (Vieille Ville). Highlights include St. Peter's Cathedral and Maison Tavel. (Free)

The cost is nothing.

Afternoon: Take a guided tour of the United Nations Office in Geneva to learn about its operations and global relevance. (Approximately CHF 12 per person)

Learn about humanitarian activities by visiting the International Red Cross and Red Crescent Museum. (Approximately CHF 15 per person)

CHF 27.00 per person

Evening: Enjoy a peaceful evening at an Old Town restaurant, eating Swiss delicacies like fondue or raclette. (Roughly CHF 30-40 per person)

Take an evening walk along Lake Geneva's gorgeous promenade and take in the city lights.

Cost per person: CHF 30-40

<u>Day 2</u>

<u>Morning</u> The Patek Philippe Museum is a horological museum that displays excellent watches. (Approximately CHF 10 per person)

Discover a large collection of art and artifacts at the Museum of Art and History. (Approximately CHF 10 per person)

CHF 20.00 per person

<u>Afternoon:</u> Enjoy a relaxing boat trip on Lake Geneva while observing the stunning sceneries and neighboring mountains. (Approximately CHF 20 per person)

Learn about the region's vegetation, animals, and geological history at the Museum of Natural History. (Approximately CHF 10 per person)

The cost is CHF 30 per participant.

<u>Evening:</u> Dine at a lakeside restaurant and soak in the atmosphere while enjoying Swiss cuisine. (Roughly CHF 40-50 per person)

Attend a classical music event or a theatrical production at one of the city's prestigious venues. (Roughly CHF 30-50 per person)

Cost per person: CHF 70-100

Day 3

Morning: Take a day excursion to Chillon Castle, a historic fortification on Lake Geneva's beaches. Explore the ancient halls and scenic surroundings. (Entry fee of around CHF 12 per person, plus transportation charges)
Cost varies based on mode of transportation.

Afternoon: Explore Geneva's Botanical Gardens, which include a broad selection of plant species and stunning sceneries. (Free)
Marvel at the Museum of Natural History's enormous collection of fossils and minerals. (Approximately CHF 10 per person) The cost is CHF 10 per participant.

Evening: Dinner at a contemporary restaurant in the Eaux-Vives district, which is noted for its dynamic eating scene. (Roughly CHF 40-50 per person)
Take a stroll along the Quai du Mont-Blanc, which overlooks the lake and provides spectacular sunset views.
Cost per person: CHF 40-50

Day 4

Morning: Explore the Ariana Museum, which is devoted to ceramics and glassware and has exhibits from many times and countries. (Approximately CHF 10 per person)
Visit the Reformation Wall, a memorial to prominent people from the Protestant Reformation. (Free)
The cost is CHF 10 per participant.

Afternoon: Take a relaxing bike ride along

Day 5

Morning: Begin your day by visiting the International Museum of the Red Cross and Red Crescent, which is close to the United Nations. Investigate the interactive exhibitions that give information on the humanitarian efforts of the organization. (Approximately CHF 15 per person)
CHF 15.00 per person

Afternoon: Take a picturesque train trip to Montreux, a lovely village on Lake Geneva's shoreline. Visit the Montreux Jazz Café to see the famed Montreux Jazz Festival posters and take a stroll along the lake promenade. (Around CHF 20 for a round-trip train ticket CHF 20.00 per person

Evening: Dinner at one of Montreux's lakeside restaurants, which provide stunning views and a wide range of cuisines. (Roughly CHF 40-50 per person)

The Château de Chillon, a historic castle near Montreux, is worth a visit. Take a guided tour to learn about its history and see the stunning views of Lake Geneva. (Entry fee of around CHF 12 per person)

Cost per person: CHF 52-62.

Day 6

Morning Explore the lovely town of Chamonix in France, noted for its spectacular views of Mont Blanc, on a day excursion to the Swiss Alps. Enjoy magnificent views of the surrounding mountains by taking a cable car journey to Aiguille du Midi. (Transportation and cable car around CHF 70-90 per person) Cost varies based on mode of transportation.

Afternoon: Hike through the Chamonix Valley and take in the stunning alpine scenery. Depending on your fitness level and tastes, you may select from a variety of paths. (Free)

Evening: Return to Geneva for supper at a charming restaurant in the city center, where you may sample Swiss specialties like or Swiss chocolate desserts. (Roughly CHF 30-40 per person)

Enjoy the nighttime views of Lake Geneva by strolling along the Quai Gustave-Ador.

Cost per person: CHF 30-40

Day 7

Morning: Return to the International Red Cross and Red Crescent Museum to see any exhibitions you missed before. (Approximately CHF 15 per person)

CHF 15.00 per person

Afternoon: Discover the Carouge district, which is noted for its lively atmosphere and lovely streets. Explore shops and art galleries while having a coffee or lunch at a neighborhood café. (Prices vary.)

Evening: Enjoy the gorgeous hues bouncing off the lake on a sunset sail on Lake Geneva. (Roughly CHF 30-40 per person)

Enjoy a goodbye supper at a great dining establishment with excellent Swiss cuisine. (Roughly CHF 70-100 per person)

Cost per person: CHF 100-140

This itinerary gives you an in-depth look into Geneva and its surroundings, enabling you to learn about the city's culture, history, environment, and gastronomic pleasures. Prices are estimates and may vary based on individual preferences and seasonal fluctuations.

Conclusion

Finally, Geneva is a remarkable location that seamlessly combines natural beauty, historical history, and a cosmopolitan ambience. This travel guide's goal was to provide you a full insight of the city, its attractions, and the experiences it has to offer.

The breathtaking setting of Geneva at the point of Lake Geneva, surrounded by the beautiful Alps, sets the scene for an amazing visit. Geneva has something for everyone, whether you want to explore the gorgeous Old Town with its lovely cobblestone alleys and ancient buildings or indulge in the city's world-class culinary scene and luxury shopping.

We have highlighted some of the must-see attractions throughout this tour, such as the famed Jet d'Eau, the grand St. Pierre Cathedral, and the Palais des Nations, where world diplomacy takes place. The city's vibrant cultural environment is also reflected in its various museums and galleries, which include the Museum of Art and History, the Red Cross Museum, and the Patek Philippe Museum.

For nature lovers, the surrounding countryside offers a plethora of outdoor activities. The area provides a varied variety of chances for discovery and adventure, from sailing on Lake Geneva to trekking in the adjacent Jura Mountains or skiing in the Alps. Furthermore, Geneva's devotion to humanitarian causes, as well as its status as a worldwide diplomatic center, making it a one-of-a-kind destination. Visitors may learn about the city's rich history and the inner workings of international organizations by taking guided tours and visiting institutions such as the United Nations Office in Geneva.

In summary, the city of Geneva's status as a gastronomic mecca should not be disregarded. The city has a thriving culinary scene, with a diverse selection of different cuisines to please every appetite. Gastronomic pleasures abound, from traditional Swiss meals to Michelin-starred restaurants and modern cafés.

As you finish this travel guide, we hope it has motivated you to start on an exciting vacation in Geneva. Whether you're attracted to Geneva for its natural beauty, cultural legacy, or international relevance, it provides a riveting mix of activities that will make an indelible impression. So pack your luggage, immerse yourself in the city's beauty, and make memories that will last long after you leave Geneva. Best wishes!

Made in the USA
Las Vegas, NV
03 September 2023

77013166R00075